W9-DGM-182

BIBLE STORY POEMS

Phil,
May God bless!

Debra
R.

BIBLE STORY POEMS

Debra Russell

WESTBOW·
PRESS
A DIVISION OF THOMAS NELSON
& ZONDERVAN

Copyright © 2014 Debra Russell.

All rights reserved. No part of this book may be used or reproduced by
any means, graphic, electronic, or mechanical, including photocopying,
recording, taping or by any information storage retrieval system
without the written permission of the publisher except in the case
of brief quotations embodied in critical articles and reviews.

The Thompson Chain Reference Bible Fifth Improved Edition- King James Version
Tyndale Life Application Bible- New International Version
The Message- Eugene H Peterson

WestBow Press books may be ordered through booksellers or by contacting:

WestBow Press
A Division of Thomas Nelson & Zondervan
1663 Liberty Drive
Bloomington, IN 47403
www.westbowpress.com
1 (866) 928-1240

Because of the dynamic nature of the Internet, any web addresses or
links contained in this book may have changed since publication and
may no longer be valid. The views expressed in this work are solely those
of the author and do not necessarily reflect the views of the publisher,
and the publisher hereby disclaims any responsibility for them.

Any people depicted in stock imagery provided by Thinkstock are models,
and such images are being used for illustrative purposes only.
Certain stock imagery © Thinkstock.

ISBN: 978-1-4908-4914-0 (sc)
ISBN: 978-1-4908-4915-7 (hc)
ISBN: 978-1-4908-4916-4 (e)

Library of Congress Control Number: 2014915606

Printed in the United States of America.

WestBow Press rev. date: 10/6/2014

Contents

New Testament

OLD TESTAMENT

Abigail - Read: I Samuel 25:1-42

When the prophet Samuel died
Israel mourned burying a great man
David arose and traveled down
To the wilderness of Paran

There lived a man named Nabal
He was a Calebite
This man was very foolish
He wouldn't do right

He married a woman named Abigail
That was beautiful and wise
While she was of good understanding
He was a man we could despise

Nabal was very wealthy
He owned three thousand sheep
He had one thousand goats
This is a lot of stock to keep

When shearing time arrived
Nabal traveled to Carmel
After David heard about the trip
He put ten men on his trail

The young men greeted Nabal
With instructions that had been given
They told Nabal about their protection
And how his shepherds were living

Ask your men and they'll tell you
What we've done for thee
You can give what you want
We come in peace you see

David runs from his master
And wants me to give to thee
Who is this David?
Who is the Son of Jesse?

I'm to take bread and water
And the meat that I have
And give to men that are hiding?
I don't want to go down that path

The young men left Nabal
They went on their way
Telling David everything
That Nabal had to say

David got very angry
Four hundred men brought their sword
There was no secret
Who they were heading toward

One of the young men
Told Nabal's wife
Nabal insulted David
He's putting an end to our life

David's men were good
They took care of us all
Protected us day and night
By creating a strong wall

No one can talk to the master
That man is mad
He doesn't do what's right
He does what is bad

Abigail made haste
Gathering a lot of stuff
Because of her husband's big mouth
Her job was very tough

She had five dressed sheep, loaves and corn
She included two bottles of wine
Raisin cakes and figs by the dozen
Everything needed to dine

Abigail told her servant
You can go before me
Nabal didn't know where she went
She didn't want him to see

While she was out riding
She came down by a hill
David and his men approached
Telling her how they feel

When Abigail saw David
She fell to her feet
She bowed to the ground
He was the one she wanted to meet

Upon me Lord
Let this iniquity be
But as for my husband Nabal
Let that man go free

Don't pay attention to him
What he did was very cruel
The meaning of his name
Should tell you he's a fool

Forgive your servant's offense
The Lord follows you
Don't let evil be found
In anything you do

David, the Lord has kept you
From bloodshed with your hand
Your enemies keep trying to hurt you
They don't understand

Please remember thy servant
When you're blessed with everything
God has already decided
That you will be Israel's King

David spoke to Abigail
Giving praises to the Lord
May you be blessed for judgment
Keeping me away from my sword

The Lord God of Israel
Kept me from harming you
If you had not met me today
Killing is what I would do

David accepted the goods
He let Abigail go
It's not who you are
Sometimes it's who you know

Abigail saw Nabal
Holding a feast for a king
Too drunk to understand
What his foolishness would bring

She explained the next day
Probably using a quiet tone
But Nabal's heart failed him
His body became as stone

Ten days later the Lord struck him
Nabal the Calebite died
David praised the Lord
That this wicked man was tried

David sent word to Abigail
Asking her to be his wife
She wasted no time
Starting her new life

Abigail and her five maidens
Followed David's messengers on an ass
She wanted to be David's wife
She didn't let opportunity pass

The Altar Challenge - Read: I Kings 18:1-45

Elijah, go see King Ahab
I am sending rain
Samaria's famine lasted three long years
The people were in pain

Elijah went to Ahab
Obadiah was called by the king
Since he was the governor
He could handle almost anything

Obadiah feared the Lord
Bread and water is what he gave
To 100 prophets that he hid
By 50 in a cave

Jezebel had cut them off
Obadiah made sure they ate
He obeyed the Living God
He wouldn't let Jezebel dictate

King Ahab told Obadiah
To check the water unto the brook
We might find grass for the mules and horses
Let's go take a look

They divided the land
They went their separate way
When Obadiah saw Elijah
This is what he had to say

Art thou my lord Elijah?
I am, go tell the king
If I go and you leave
I can suffer for this thing

I will not leave
I will meet him this day
Obadiah told the king
So he came to have his say

Are you troubling Israel?
No! You are breaking God's command
Since you are worshipping Baalim
Your fate is in his hand

Tell Israel to come
To a mount called Carmel
Let's see if Baalim is great
Or what he has to sell

Ahad called the Children of Israel
And the Prophets of Baal
These men got together
Not intending to fail

Elijah asked the people
How long will you try to serve two?
If God is your god follow him
What are you trying to do?

If you follow Baal
Go make him your lord
Trying to serve them both
Is something we can't afford

The people did not speak
After Elijah finished his speech
I would have probably wondered
How many did I reach?

Elijah represented God
450 Prophets represented Baal
Provide two bulls for the sacrifice
Let's see who is going to fail

Let them pick a bull
Cut it up, lay it on the wood
They can't add fire
But let's see if Baalim could

The prophets prepared the bull
Calling from morning till noon
They sent praises to Baal
With hope that he would answer soon

They hopped around the altar
Singing praises to him
He didn't say a word
He wouldn't answer them

It was almost noon
Elijah said, shout louder!
Perhaps he is sleeping or busy
You need to make him prouder

The prophets start shouting
Running around cutting their skin
Blood start gushing all over
These wicked men

The prophets continued
Until the Offering of Oblation
They never received a word
This brought about frustration

Elijah spoke to the people
Come close to me
He repaired God's altar
With 12 stones for the family

Each stone represented a tribe
To whom God said, Israel's your name
God strengthens people
Let's learn to do the same

Elijah made a deep trench
Around the altar that day
He showed all of the people
That God's the only way

He put the wood in order
Laying the bull on top of it
You will not believe
What he asked the people to get

Bring four barrels of water
Drench this sacrifice
They did this three times
Following his advice

At the time of Oblation
Elijah spoke to the Lord
Because of his dedication
They knew who he looked toward

Answer My Lord, answer me
So the people will know it's you
So they will turn their hearts back
And do what they need to do

Then the fire of the Lord
Consumed the offering on the ground
It lapped up all the water
There was nothing left around

After the people saw this
They fell upon their face
Praising the Living God
Giving honor and receiving grace

Elijah told the people
Seize the Prophets of Baal
Don't let them escape
They serve the god that fail

The prophets were taken to the brook
They were all killed
This was necessary
So that the people could be healed

Elijah told King Ahab
Get up, drink and eat
I hear the sound of rain
God's blessing is complete

After the king left
To do what Elijah said
Elijah went to the mountaintop
Got on his knees and bowed his head

He told his servant
Look toward the sea
The servant seeing nothing
Wondered what should this be?

The servant checked seven times
And the last time that he went
A cloud rose like a man's hand
God's blessing had been sent

Meanwhile the sky grew dark
With clouds and lots of wind
The rain had start falling
That God promised to send

Balaam's Donkey - Read: Numbers 22

In the plains of Moab
Dwelled the Israelites
King Balak feared these people
Because they destroyed the Amorites

The Israelites are many
Their numbers are not small
If we don't defeat them
They will kill us all

He sent messengers to Balaam
Telling him to talk to the Lord
Put a curse on these people
A disaster's something I can't afford

The Elders of Midian and Moab
Departed with rewards in hand
Balaam agreed to speak to God
About what King Balak planned

You are welcome to lodge here
You are welcome to stay
The Lord will speak to me tonight
He will show me the way

God came unto Balaam
Who are these men with thee?
They want me to curse Israel
They brought a divination fee

Balaam rose the next morning
Saying, take leave to your land
God will not agree
To what you have planned

The men returned to Balak
Balaam will not come
I will send greater than you
Carrying a larger sum

Balaam greeted the men
It doesn't matter what you give
God will not curse His people
He wants them to live

Tarry ye also this night
God may have more to say
God told Balaam if they call
You can follow them on their way

But Balaam rose the next morning
Doing what he wanted to do
Some people are led by self
Don't let this be you

After Balaam got up
He saddled his ass
The animal saw an angel with a sword
That wouldn't let her pass

The donkey turned aside
Going into a field
Balaam smote the animal
Demanding that she yield

She saw the Angel of the Lord again
So she crushed Balaam's foot against a wall
Balaam smote her again
Not seeing the angel at all

The Angel of the Lord went further
Standing in a narrow place
The ass saw the angel again
Knowing what she had to face

After seeing the angel once more
She fell to the ground
Balaam got upset and smote her
Thinking she was fooling around

The Lord opened her mouth
She asked Balaam, what have I done to thee?
You didn't strike a few times
You had to hit me three

Balaam told the donkey
You refused to do what I said
If I had a sword in hand
My donkey would be dead

The animal told Balaam
Unto this day I've done all you said
Then the Lord opened Balaam's eyes
He fell flat and bowed his head

Why did you smite this ass?
She was obeying me
She was trying to protect you
Because I would have killed thee

Balaam said to the angel
I'm committing sin
I didn't see you standing there
I can go back home again

The angel said to Balaam
Follow those men on their way
I will give you the words
I will tell you what to say

King Balak said to Balaam
I was earnest when I sent for thee
I could've promoted you to honor
But you wouldn't come see me

Lo I come to you
But I can't speak a thing
God's put in my mouth
The words that I will sing

Balaam followed Balak
He took him to the high place
Where he saw God's people
And all he had to face

Cain and Abel - Read: Genesis 4:2-17

Abel was a keeper of sheep
Cain tilled the ground
God gives different professions
When passing his gifts around

This story's about two brothers
That brought God a sacrifice
God respected Abel's
Cain's was not so nice

God told Cain to do well
And I will accept you
But if you continue like this
Sinning is what you'll do

Cain was talking to Abel
While they were in the field
Cain got very angry
And his brother was killed

God asked Cain
Where is your brother?
I don't know, why ask me?
Am I the keeper of another?

What have you done?
Your brother's blood cries from the ground
God had warned Cain
That sin was lurking around

Cain you are cursed
The ground will not give you her yield
It's receiving your brother's blood
While he lies dead in the field

My punishment is more
Than I can ever bare
People will try to slay me
I don't think that's fair

You will be alright
Listen to what I say
Anyone trying to slay you
Will have a price to pay

God put a mark on Cain
Vengeance shall be sevenfold
No one will try to slay you
That would be bold

Cain left God's presence
Moved to Nod and knew his wife
She bared their son Enoch
This begins their life

Daniel in the Lion's Den - Read: Daniel 6:3-26

Daniel from the tribe of Judah
Faithful as can be
Was preferred by King Darius
Over the Princes and Presidency

These men were jealous of Daniel
Daniel's taking over everything
We need to bring him down
Let's do it by using our King

Daniel is so upright
It will be hard to find anything wrong
He serves a God over Israel
They say He's very strong

I have seen Daniel praying
To his God above
Let's use it against him
That he shows his God love

He prays to his God
Three times a day
If we tell King Darius
What do you think he'll say?

We can make a decree
Prayer for thirty days is not allowed
Only show the King honor
Because this makes him proud

The King signed the decree
That giving honor was a sin
If you broke the decree
You were tossed in the lion's den

These men went looking for Daniel
They found him on the floor
We know you were honoring your God
We don't need to see anymore

King Darius, Daniel is praying
He kneels three times a day
He's ignoring everything
That you had to say

We know that you love Daniel
But you can't change this decree
You must put him in the lion's den
This man will not go free

The king had no choice
He did what the men said
He couldn't eat or enjoy music that night
He laid restless on his bed

He remembered telling Daniel
Before tonight is through
I know the God you serve
Is going to deliver you

The king rose the next morning
He went to the lion's den
Did your God save you Daniel?
What shape are you in?

Oh king live forever
My God delivered me
His angel came and shut their mouth
So the king set Daniel free

Daniel was taken out
The evil men were cast down
Their families were eaten that day
Their bones were broken before hitting the ground

King Darius was very happy
The decree had this to say
Daniel's God is the one to serve
There is no other way

David and Bathsheba - Read: II Samuel 11- 12:24

King David stayed in Jerusalem
While his army went out to fight
They defeated the Children of Ammon
Why didn't David do right?

One evening while at the palace
David rose from off his bed
While walking on his roof top
A thought entered his head

He saw a beautiful woman
His eyes were filled with lust
She was washing her body
Having her was a must

I want to meet that woman
They knew who he talked about
I want her to come to me
So he sent some messengers out

When Bathsheba arrived
David slept with her
She had completed her purification
Let me tell you what's going to occur

Bathsheba will send the message
I am having your kid
David will respond quickly
Knowing what he did

He sent a message to Joab
Send Uriah the Hittite to me
David tried to deceive Bathsheba's husband
So life would go smoothly

The King spoke to Uriah
Go home and wash your feet
Uriah stayed with the King's servants
My wife's not the one I will greet

The next day David asked Uriah
Why didn't you go to your house?
While the men are fighting a battle
I can't enjoy my spouse

As surely as you live
I would do no such thing
David invited him two more days
To see what it would bring

Uriah ate and drank with the King
David got him very drunk
He still didn't go to his house
What David did really stunk

So David gave Uriah a letter for Joab
Put Uriah on the front line
The letter stated that if Uriah dies
It will be just fine

Joab followed instructions
Doing what he had to do
He put Uriah on the front line
And then the men withdrew

Uriah the Faithful Hittite
Died on that day
The messenger gave a report
This is what he had to say

They met us in the field
We pursued them to the gate
The shooters shot from the wall
A few men met their fate

David told the messenger
Joab shouldn't be so upset
The sword's a devourer
Wounding who it can get

After Bathsheba was told
She grieved for her spouse
David married the woman
Moving her into his house

David had did something
That no one could afford
He had upset
And displeased the Lord

The Lord sent Nathan
To talk to David the King
Nathan told him a story
To see the reaction it would bring

This story's about a rich man
And a man that was poor
The rich man stole the poor man's lamb
Because he wanted more

He stole the little ewe lamb
That this poor man had
When Nathan finished the story
David was very mad

That man should die
That did this awful thing
Then you are guilty
This was done by our King

The Lord told me to tell you
What you did wasn't right
You are despised
The sword will not depart from your sight

Evil will arise
From your house
The neighbors will sleep with women
That are your spouse

You did this in secret
But I will make Israel see
You broke my commandments
You have despised me

David made a confession
I have committed sin
David finally realized
How wicked he had been

God will not kill you
He will pardon what you did
You will suffer loss
He is going to take your kid

Within seven days
David's child was ill
Bathsheba's baby was the one
That the Lord was going to kill

David prayed for the baby
David began a fast
The Elders were probably wondering
How long will this last?

Nathan went home
David prayed on the ground
After seven days
The baby wasn't around

After the baby's death
The Elders wondered what to do
The servant had to tell the King
Your child has left you

David saw them whispering
The thought entered his head
So he asked the question
Is my baby dead?

David got up after hearing the news
And made himself neat
He worshipped God
They gave him food to eat

The servants couldn't understand
Why the King was ok
When the baby died
David had this to say

While my child lived
God might give me grace
I fasted and I wept
For what I had to face

Now the child is gone
I can't bring him back
One day I will see him
So what will I lack?

David comforted Bathsheba
She bare him another son
The Lord loved the baby
That he called "Solomon"

David and Goliath - Read: I Samuel 17:4-51

Goliath a Philistine giant
Boasted for forty days
He frightened Israel's army
In so many ways

The warrior was very big
He was nine foot nine
The army wouldn't fight him
They didn't cross that line

He wore a brass helmet
He was armed with a coat of mail
He had brass all over
As far as I could tell

He taunted them twice a day
Saying, get someone I can fight
The men didn't want to die
They were afraid of Goliath's height

When I defeat you
You will be our slaves
This was the kind of speech
That Goliath gave

If you can defeat us
Let me tell you what we will do
We will be your slaves
We will serve you

The head on Goliath's spear
Was like a weaver's beam
The Philistines knew they could win
With Goliath on their team

Jesse had eight sons
Only three fought in the war
When David was asked to deliver food
He knew who it was for

David was a shepherd
With a flock to keep
While he made the delivery
Someone else watched his sheep

He woke early in the morning
Loading up his cart
With cheese, bread and corn
He was trying to do his part

After David arrived
He heard what Goliath said
Then he found out that King Saul
Wanted this giant dead

David asked around
What would be the reward
For taking away Israel's reproach
And restoring the Army of the Lord?

That man would be rich
He would marry the daughter of Saul
That man's family would not pay
To live in Israel at all

David asked the king
Who is this uncircumcised Philistine?
God delivered me from a lion and bear
When they stepped out of line

The king gave David his armor
It was hard to move around
If he stayed in this outfit
He would end up on the ground

David removed the armor
He used what he brought
David carried a staff
And he had his sling shot

Goliath was not prepared
For the weapons that David would pick
The giant became angry
When he saw him with his stick

Am I but a dog?
That you would treat me this way
The beast and fowls will eat your flesh
On this very day

David was very comfortable
With the weapons that he took
He picked up five smooth stones
That were lying in the brook

David said I see your sword
You brought your spear and shield
But I'm bringing the Lord of Host
Your fate is now sealed

The Philistine got up
He advanced after hearing what David said
David put a stone in a sling
Hitting Goliath in the head

Goliath fell on his face
David took the giant's sword
He cut off Goliath's head
To receive his great reward

When the Philistine's saw
That their champion was dead
They wasted no time
All of the men fled

Deborah and Barak - Read: Judges 4, 5:2

Deborah was a judge
She spent time under a tree
Administering God's Word
The way that it should be

She sent for Barak
Reminding him of what God said
But Barak feared Sisera
He couldn't get him out of his head

I will not fight the Mighty Sisera
Unless you go with me
Deborah decided to go
So that Israel would be free

You won't receive the honor
It's something you can't demand
Sisera will be delivered by a woman
The matters out of your hand

Sisera gathered his army
Barak's the one I want to meet
But when the Lord discomforted him
Sisera fled on his feet

Barak pursued the army
Killing them with his sword
Having freedom in Israel
Will be a great reward

Sisera fled to Jael
The wife of Heber the Kenite
Since there was peace with Jabin the King
He thought he'd be alright

Jael went out to meet him
Saying, come turn in to me
She covered him with a mantle
So that others would not see

He told her he was thirsty
She gave him a bottle of milk
Tell them you haven't seen me
His plan was smooth as silk

Sisera fell asleep
Jael heard all that he said
But she took a nail with a hammer
And drove it in his head

Barak pursued Sisera
Jael wanted to make life simple
Follow me and I'll show you the man
With a nail in his temple

Deborah and Barak sang a song
Our enemy has been defeated
By obeying God's instructions
The victory was completed

Deception in Eden - Read: Genesis 3:1-19

Eve was in the garden
Talking to the serpent one day
About a tree in the midst
That was standing near her way

The serpent spoke to her
Giving some advice
He was very cunning
What he said was not nice

Didn't the Lord say
Don't eat of every tree
We can eat from them all
Except the one that you see

If we eat or touch it
We will surely die
That is not true
And I do not lie

God knows when you eat from it
You will be like Him
Knowing good and evil
Will not put you on the limb

When the woman saw
That the tree would make her wise
She gave some to her husband
This will open up our eyes

The first thing that they saw
Was that they needed clothes
They made them out of leaves
The way the story goes

They heard God's voice
In the cool of the day
When they hid themselves
He had this to say

Where art thou?
We are naked you see
How do you know?
You didn't get that from me

We hid ourselves
Because we were afraid
We didn't obey You
A bad choice has been made

The woman that you gave me
That was very sweet
Gave me fruit
I wasn't supposed to eat

God asked Eve
What have you done?
I was beguiled
Yes, the serpent was the one

Serpent, you are cursed
Above all the beast around
You will go on your belly
In the dust on the ground

There will be enmity
Between your and her seed
There was a penalty
For his wicked deed

It shall bruise thy head
Thou shall bruise his heel
After receiving this punishment
How would a serpent feel?

Sorrow will be multiplied
When the woman brings forth a child
Her desire is to please her husband
Since she was beguiled

Then God told Adam
Since you hearkened to your wife
The ground will be cursed
All the days of your life

In the sweat of thy face
Thou shall eat bread
The couple heard everything
That the Lord said

You were made from dust
That was taken from the ground
Some day to return
From where you were found

Elijah - Read: I Kings 17:1-22

Elijah told King Ahab
The Lord's not providing rain
This judgment brings suffering
And you know there will be pain

The Word of God came to Elijah
Hide yourself by a brook
I've commanded the ravens to bring flesh and bread
You won't have to look

The ravens were very faithful
They brought this meal at night
Elijah didn't worry about tomorrow
They brought more when it was light

God supplied the water
Elijah lived by the brook
After sometime the brook dried up
From the water that he took

The Lord told him to go to Zarephath
A widow will sustain thee
When he arrived in the city he told her
Please fetch some water for me

As she went to fetch it
He said, bring a morsel in hand
After he asked this favor
She decided to share her plan

I have some meal in a barrel
A little oil in a cruse
I'm going to make, my son and I a cake
These are the items that I will use

You see, this country was having a drought
The widow and her son were about to die
Just watch and see what God will do
He will increase her supply

Go and do as you said
But first make a cake for me
My God is about to bless you
He will multiply abundantly

The widow made his cake
Her meal and oil failed her not
The widow and her son ate for many days
Wouldn't you want to be in her spot?

Sometime after these things
The widow's son died
Were her sins being remembered?
Was this woman being tried?

Elijah took the boy to his room
Laying him on his bed
He stretched across him three times praying
And this is what he said

Have thou brought evil
To this widow's son?
The soul of the youth was restored
Look at what the Lord has done

Ezekiel's Dry Bone Experience - Read: Ezekiel 37:1-14

Ezekiel was in the midst
Of bones that were very dry
What does this really say
About you and I?

The hand of the Lord was upon me
It took me where it wanted to go
A valley full of dry bones
To a place I did not know

Bones were all around me
They were everywhere
God asked me a question
That was too much for me to bear

Can these bones live?
Lord only you would know
I want you to prophesy
Let me tell you how this will go

I'm the Lord your God
Breath is what I'll give
You will not remain dry
You will surely live

After that I prophesied
Doing as I was told
I witnessed great works
That were very bold

Then I heard a noise
It was a shaking sound
The bones were coming together
That were lying on the ground

While I continued watching
They received flesh and skin
They were not yet breathing
What kind of state were they in?

The Lord said to me
Prophesy unto the breath
These bones will live
That were put to death

Breath, come from four winds
Breathe into the slain
Restore their bodies
Before they received their pain

I prophesied to them
Using the Lord's name
Breath entered their bodies
They were not the same

The men came to life
Standing on their feet
I saw a vast army
God's work was complete

God said to me
The bones represent Israel
I am the "Redeemer"
Rescuing them from their jail

Let my people know
I will open up their grave
They will return home
To the land that I gave

Then the people will know
That I am the Lord
I will put my Spirit in them
To live in one accord

The Fiery Furnace - Read: Daniel 3

King Nebuchadnezzar made an idol
The image was made out of gold
He didn't serve the Living God
This is the way the story's told

Everyone in my kingdom
Shall bow down to the sound
When the instruments start playing
They will fall on the ground

Three Jewish men wouldn't listen
Their names I'm sure you will know
The king said, obey my decree
Shadrach, Meshach and Abed-nego

I will throw you in the furnace
Listen to what I say
It will burn seven times hotter
Ignore me and you will pay

Our God will deliver us
If it is in His will
We will not worship your idol
This is how we feel

You are going in the furnace
My men will throw you in
The flame reached out and slew the guards
Trying to commit that sin

The Hebrew boys were bound
And thrown into a burning flame
We only threw in three men
What is the fourth one's name?

The fourth is like the Son of God
The boys are not alone
We put them in to do them harm
I don't even hear a moan

Come out of the fiery furnace
There is a new decree
Anyone talking against your God
Has to contend with me

Shadrach, Meshach and Abed-nego
Were promoted on that day
This story has a happy ending
Serving God's the only way

Gideon - Read: Judges 6:1-24

The Children of Israel
Had been stripped of their rights
They've suffered seven years
To the Midianites

The Midianites came in numbers
They took their animals and crop
They showed no compassion
They didn't know when to stop

God had warned Israel
I'm with you when you obey
But they wouldn't listen
They just went their own way

After being made poor
They cried out to the Lord
God sent them a Prophet
Reminding them of what they ignored

An angel spoke to Gideon
While he was threshing wheat
Gideon was hiding behind the winepress
So he would have food to eat

Mighty man of valour
The Lord is with thee
Then why has this befallen us
In the land that you see?

Where are the miracles
That our Fathers talked about?
We are serving the Midianites
Where is our out?

The Lord told Gideon
If you go in thy might
You can save Israel
From the Midianites

How can I save them?
My family is very poor
I will go with you
I can open any door

You can smite them
As one man
If anyone can do this
I know that you can

Lord if in thy sight
I have found grace
Show me a sign
That we spoke in this place

Do not depart
Until I come back to thee
I have a gift for you
Ok, I will tarry

Gideon left to prepare a kid
And some unleavened cake
He was happy to do it
For the Lord's sake

He put flesh in a basket
And broth in a pot
The angel was waiting under an oak tree
In the same spot

Take the flesh and cake
Put them upon this rock
The next thing he told him
Was to pour out the stock

The Angel of the Lord
Put forth the staff in his hand
Fire consumed the offering
Now Gideon could understand

The Lord said to Gideon
Peace be unto thee
Thou shall not die
Because you saw me

Gideon built an altar
It's called Jehovah-shalom unto this day
God answers questions
Choose to obey

Hannah - Read: I Samuel 1

Elkanah from Mount Ephraim
Had two wives
This is a perfect example
Of how we complicate our lives

Peninnah had children
She had more than a few
Since Hannah was barren
She didn't know what to do

Every year Elkanah
Went to worship and sacrifice
When he handed out portions
Hannah's was very nice

Elkanah loved his wife Hannah
But she couldn't have a child
Her adversary provoked her sorely
She was taunted and she was riled

Hannah was unable to eat
All she did was cry
Out of concern for his wife
Elkanah wanted to know why

Hannah, am I not better
Than ten boys?
This woman had been robbed
Of all of her joys

Hannah went to the temple
Giving her burdens to the Lord
Eli thought she was drunk
This is something she couldn't afford

How long will you drink?
Woman, put away your wine
Eli was talking to her
Trying to get her in line

I am not drunk
Do you think me a daughter of Belial?
I'm sharing my sorrowful spirit
With a God that will never fail

Eli told Hannah
Hannah, go in peace
God will grant your petition
His blessings will never cease

Then Hannah replied
Let me find grace in thy sight
She started eating and drinking
She was a changed woman that night

Early the very next morning
The family returned to their house
Hannah spent some special time
With her devoted spouse

God remembered Hannah
She conceived a son
This woman was barren
Look what God has done

Hannah made a vow
A razor will not touch his head
She would bring him to the temple
Doing all that she said

She named the boy Samuel
Because he was asked of the Lord
God answered Hannah's prayers
This couldn't be ignored

Hannah wanted to wean the child
Before taking him to the Lord
Giving him back to God
Was something she could afford

After Samuel was weaned
She took him to the temple
With three bullocks, flour and wine in hand
Her task was very simple

They slew a bull
And brought Samuel to Eli
Hannah said to him
I was the one to testify

One day I came to the temple
On a powerful mission
I asked the Lord for this child
He has granted my petition

I prayed to God
He has answered me
I'm returning Samuel to The Lord
I've been blessed abundantly

Isaiah's Experience - Read: Isaiah 6: 1-8

The year that King Uzziah died
I was blessed to see the Lord
He sat high upon a throne
A vision I could not afford

The Lord's train was so long
It filled the temple
Nothing that I witnessed that day
Could be called simple

The seraphims stood above
With a total of six wings
Singing praises to the Lord
The Almighty King of kings

Two wings covered their face
While two covered their feet
The other set was used for flight
This was very neat

One seraphim cried to another
Holy, Holy, Holy
This whole earth
Is filled with His glory

The post of the door
Moved at His voice
This was truly amazing
A time to rejoice

The entire house
Was filled with smoke
I saw all of this
After the seraphim had spoke

Then I replied
Woe is me
I am undone
In this place that I see

My lips were not clean
Nor were any in the land
Since the Lord is a provider
He could understand

So one of His seraphim
Flew unto me
Bringing a live coal
To remove my iniquity

Tongs were used
Brought from the holy place
The coal touched my mouth
My sins were erased

I heard the Lord say
Who will go for us?
This was something
That I was ready to discuss

I stepped forward
Now that I could see
I told the Lord
You can send me

Jacob's Ladder - Read: Genesis 28:10-22

Jacob left Beersheba
Approaching a place called Haran
He spent the night in peace
Jacob was a traveling man

After the sun set
He made a pillow out of stone
Jacob laid down to rest
Thinking he was alone

While he laid sleeping
He saw a ladder reaching from Heaven to Earth
Angels were ascending and descending
What could this vision be worth?

The Lord of Abraham and Isaac
Stood above the ladder
Promising Jacob all of the land
This could really matter

Jacob's seed would be multiplied
Like the dust of the earth
The only one who could make this promise
Is the God that gave him birth

Through Jacob's Family
The whole earth would be blessed
This gift could be received
Once a sinner confessed

God will not leave me
He will be where ever I go
And would bring me back again
To this place that I know

Jacob woke up and replied
I didn't know the Lord was in this place
Jacob had just experienced
God's saving grace

He was very afraid
How dreadful is this place
This is God's house
I'm in a holy space

If this is His house
I have seen heaven's gate
Jacob rose up early
He could no longer wait

He took the stone
Setting it up as a pillar
He anointed it with oil
Because he knew God was a healer

Jacob called the place Bethel
And then he made a vow
If God be with me in everything
I will follow Him now

Jacob wanted to go home
Make peace with his brother
He wanted them to live
And respect one another

Everything God gives me
I will give a tenth part
Jacob showed respect
For God was in his heart

Journey to the Promised Land - Read: Numbers 16, 17:13

Now Korah, Dathan, Abiram and On
Felt they had something to say
God uses more than you and Aaron
We will show you another way

We have two hundred and fifty Princes
With reputations that are well known
Why are we exalting you
By putting you upon a throne?

You've taken so much upon you
Who do you think you are?
All of us are holy
What have you done so far?

After Moses heard
He fell upon his face
He told Korah and his company
To bring censers to the holy place

Put fire on those censers
Let our Lord choose
If God is not pleased with this
You are going to lose

It seemeth a small thing
That your service is for the Lord
But now you envy Aaron
Have you become bored?

Moses called Dathan and Abiram
These men would not come
You want to kill us in this wilderness
The promised land is where were from

You've taken so much upon you
Who do you think you are?
We left a land of milk and honey
What have you done for us so far?

Lord, respect not their offerings
What could I possibly say?
I have not taken a thing from them
These men don't want to obey

The Glory of the Lord appeared
To the whole congregation
Moses, Aaron get away from these men
There's going to be a mass annihilation

Moses and Aaron fell on their faces
Must all die because of one man's sin?
Well, tell the congregation to get away
From these wicked men

The people listen to Moses
Doing all that he said
The ground opened up her mouth
Most of these families are dead

A fire came from God
Consuming two hundred and fifty men
The censers were made into plates for the altar
As a reminder of that sin

The next day the people murmured
Moses and Aaron killed those men
The Lord told Moses get away from these people
They will die because of this sin

Aaron took a censer
Rushing through the crowd
Trying to stop a plague
That God's wrath had allowed

By the time it was over
Fourteen thousand seven hundred had died
Our God requires dedication
Are you on the Lord's side?

The instructions were detailed
That Moses received from God
Each tribe would take time
To write their name upon a rod

Rods were taken to the tabernacle
The people would know God's choice
When God makes His decision
You don't have a voice

Aaron's rod produced fruit
God's choice was very clear
The tabernacle would be a place
That the people would always fear

King Josiah - Read: II Kings 22, 23:28

When Josiah was eight
He was king of the land
He led the people back
To obeying God's holy plan

The people worshipped idols
They did what they wanted to do
King Josiah served the Living God
Like we all should do

His father was very evil
Leading the people astray
Like his predecessors
He worshipped idols in every way

Josiah did things right
He served God with love
Repairing the damaged temple
For our Father above

While checking on the silver
Hilkiah found a book
He gave it to Shaphan
So that he could take a look

Shaphan reported to the king
About the silver that they had
To repair the temple's breaches
Because they looked so bad

While in the house
He found a book to read
It provided God's law
This is something that we need

Shaphan read to the king
The king rent his clothes
We need to obey God
I'm sure that everybody knows

Go inquire of the Lord
About the words in this book
We need to learn
About the God that we forsook

They went to Huldah
She was a Prophetess
They needed help
Getting out of this mess

She told them all
What God had said
This judgment's on the people
Not on your king's head

The people are disobeying
They do this to God's face
He's bringing judgment
Upon this wicked place

But to the king of Judah
That sent you to me
He will not suffer loss
Because I've heard his plea

His heart is so tender
He will go to his grave in peace
But my wrath on this place
Is not going to cease

The king held a meeting
To turn things around
He crushed all of the idols
He burnt them to the ground

He slew all of the priests
In the high places
He eliminated witchcraft
This king left no traces

No king before him
Turned to God with their heart
Josiah was very devoted
Making sure he did his part

Josiah kept the Passover
It's a story the people knew
A time of thanksgiving
Celebrated by every Jew

God planned to remove Judah
Out of His sight
Because of provocations
Manasseh had not done right

We know that King Josiah
Had to die some day
He worked hard with God's people
Doing things the right way

Naaman the Leper - Read: II Kings 5

Naaman a Captain in Syria
Was honored before the King
God gave him the victory
Praising Naaman was a normal thing

After the battle was won
Captives were taken from the land
Naaman was given a young maiden
That gave his wife a hand

You see Naaman was a leper
His skin was white as snow
Leprosy is a horrible disease
That limits where you go

It is hard on the body
A leper's a horrible sight
The maid knew a Prophet of God
That could make everything right

After the maid told her mistress
The King of Syria wrote a letter
He asked the King of Israel
To make his servant better

The King read the letter
Then he rent his clothes
I can't make a man live or die
This is something everybody knows

Elisha told the King
Send Captain Naaman to me
He will learn about a Prophet of God
That will set his problem free

Naaman went to Elisha's house
He stood at the Prophet's door
A messenger told him to wash in the River Jordan
But Naaman had expected more

I thought Elisha would come out
Call his God's name
But he said to dip in Jordan seven times
Is this why I came?

Abana and Pharpar are rivers in Damascus
Why can't I dip in them?
Chances of going to Jordan
Are very slim

Naaman was very upset
His servants started to talk
Naaman would've cut off his blessing
If he had decided to walk

He dipped in Jordan seven times
This man came up clean
His skin was as a young child
This was a beautiful scene

He returned to Elisha
Praising the Living God
Never experiencing this
In all the paths that he had trod

Here's a blessing from thy servant
I have gold and silver with me
Here are ten garments for you
I want to bless abundantly

As the Lord liveth
Before whom I stand
I will not take a thing
That's in your hand

Elisha, please take it
It is what I want to do
The Lord has healed me
And I want to bless you

I will not take from you
My Lord has healed thee
There is no one like my God
I'm sure that you can see

My Master worships Rimmon
Lord pardon me on this thing
I have to go and assist him
Since he is The King

Naaman go in peace
I hear what you say
Naaman left Elisha
Only traveling a little way

Gehazi Elisha's servant
Came up with a wicked plan
He wanted Naaman to pay
So he caught up with the man

All is well was the greeting
Exchanged between the two
My Master instructed me
To get some stuff from you

Sons of the Prophets from Ephraim
Are coming on this day
Give me two garments and silver
And I will be on my way

Be content, take two talent of silver
And here are two changes of clothes
Naaman was happy to help Gehazi
The way the story goes

Gehazi told his two servants
To carry it to the tower
See how people act
When they think that they have power

Elisha asked Gehazi
Where have you been?
I didn't go anywhere
Knowing he had committed sin

Gehazi my heart was with thee
Was it time for silver or gold?
Gehazi tried to get all that he could
What he did was very bold

The leprosy on Naaman the Syrian
Is going to cleave
Now it's part of your house
It's not going to leave

Gehazi walked away a leper
His skin was white as snow
This is a warning to us
That we will reap what we sow

Noah's Ark - Read: Genesis 6:13-9:16

God asked Noah to build an ark
He told him how long and wide
You will obey instructions
When on the Lord's side

He brought in animals two by two
Of the clean he brought seven
They would be used for the sacrifice
To our Father in heaven

God said that His Spirit
Would only dwell one hundred and twenty years
Since Noah chose to do what was right
He did not suffer fears

Noah had three sons
Japheth, Shem and Ham
He put his confidence in God
Better known as the great "I AM"

God shut the doors of the ark
It rained forty days
Noah's family lived, they didn't drown
Serving God really pays

Noah opened a window
Letting a raven go
While waiting for the earth to dry
The bird flew to and fro

Sending something else
He released a dove
The bird didn't find rest for her feet
So she returned to the ark of love

Sending her again
She returned with a branch from an olive tree
Once the water leaves the earth
We can all roam free

He sent her again
She returned to him no more
This is good news
Soon we can walk out the door

God spoke to Noah
Go forth with your sons and their wives
I have made big plans
You are starting new lives

Noah got off the ark
He made a sacrifice
Having a new beginning
Was going to be nice

God made a covenant
By putting a rainbow in the sky
I will not flood the earth
So that all men die.

Nothing New: The Wisdom of Solomon - Read: Ecclesiastes 1

A Preacher, The Son of David
Solomon the King
Is sharing wisdom with us
On what life will bring

Worthless, so very worthless
All that we see
Everything is vanity
Take it from me

What does a man gain
After toiling in the sun?
Do generations receive credit
For what they have done?

While generations come
And while generations go
The earth remains forever
I just thought I'd let you know

The sun also rises
And then it goes down
It hastens to a rising place
Back to where it's found

The wind goes south
And then it turns north
It does this continually
Going back and forth

All rivers run
Straight to the sea
But it doesn't overflow
Take it from me

Then the rivers return
From whence they came
They go back again
And remain the same

Everything is so wearisome
You will get worn out
What more can be said
This is what life's about

The eye never sees enough
Did the ear get it's fill?
What has been will be again
It's all so very real

For there's nothing new
Under the sun
Everything that happens
Has already been done

Is there a thing, which you can say
Look this is new?
Believe me it has happened
This shouldn't surprise you

There is no memory
Of old men or those of new
Do they expect us to remember
All the things that they do?

I was Teacher and King
Over Israel in Jerusalem
I devoted my time exploring
The subject of wisdom

What a heavy burden
God has placed upon men
I've seen everything under the sun
It's all just chasing the wind

What's twisted can't be straightened
What's lacking can't be counted
I've grown and increased in wisdom
To what has this amounted?

With wisdom comes much sorrow
The more knowledge, the more grief
God provides for tomorrow
Supplying comfort and relief

Offering Isaac - Read: Genesis 22:1-14

God told Abraham
Take Isaac thy son
Offer him as a burnt offering
I Am your number one

Abraham was very faithful
Rising early the next day
He took his son and two young men
Preparing to obey

After traveling three days
They saw the place from afar
Isaac and I will worship
You both stay where you are

He gave Isaac the wood
He carried the fire and the knife
He knew what he had to do
He had to end his son's life

Isaac spoke to his father
Father here I am
I see the wood and a knife
But where is the lamb?

Abraham told Isaac
Our God will provide
They continued on their journey
Walking side by side

After they arrived
At the chosen place
Abraham built an altar
Knowing what he had to face

He laid Isaac on the wood
Took hold of the knife
He was ready to put an end
To his son's life

The Angel of the Lord
Called Abraham's name
The instructions that were given
Would not be the same

Do not lay a hand
On your only son
I see that you've made me
Your number One

Abraham looked up
Behold there was a ram
God's a provider
He gave us His Son "The Lamb"

Abraham offered the ram
As a sacrifice
Not killing Isaac
Is going to be nice

Abraham called the place
Jehovah-jireh
This is what it's called
To this very day

Our Lord and Savior Jesus Christ - Read: Isaiah 53

Who believes our report?
Does anyone know what God's revealing?
Growing before Him, as a tender plant
He was not appealing

He was as a root
In a dry parched ground
There was no attraction to Him
Beauty could not be found

Despised and rejected
He was acquainted with grief
Carrying around our sorrows
This man had no relief

We esteemed him stricken
Was He smitten by God?
Wounded and afflicted
Because of the paths that we trod

Pierced for our transgressions
Crushed because of our sin
Punished that we may have peace
His stripes provided healing within

Like wandering sheep
We have all gone astray
While walking our own path
We are going the wrong way

God has placed all
Of our sins upon Him
Yes, He has gathered
Every one of them

Tormented and beaten
But He didn't say a word
Like a lamb lead to be slaughtered
This is what occurred

He was oppressed and judged
And then led away
Will He be remembered
While leaving the living today?

He made a grave with the wicked
And with the rich
There was no deceit in His mouth
No, not a stitch

It pleased the Lord to bruise Him
He was put to grief
His soul was offered for our sins
So that we could have relief

God will see His seed
And He will prolong His days
The pleasure of the Lord
Will prosper through His ways

Seeing His soul travail
God will be satisfied
His righteous servant is bearing our sins
So that many are justified

He'll receive a great reward
And share it with the strong
Because He was our sacrifice
He'll be numbered with the wrong

While barring the sins of many
He made intercession for us
He's Our Lord and Saviour
The only one that's Just

Sodom and Gomorrah - Read: Genesis 18, 19

The Lord said to Abraham
Shall I hide that which I do?
You will be a mighty nation
The earth will be blessed because of you

You will instruct your children
To do things the Lord's way
So the Lord can bring to Abraham
That which He has to say

The outcry against Sodom and Gomorrah
Is indeed very great
I'm going to go down
And make a decision on their fate

The angels turned their faces
They started to head toward
That place called Sodom and Gomorrah
While Abraham spoke to the Lord

Will you destroy the righteous
With the wicked in that land?
Will all men die
After you've done what you've planned?

If you can find fifty
In the city tonight
Can the Judge of all
Do what is right?

If I can find fifty
I will spare it for their sake
Can I speak Lord
I have a request to make?

If the city lacks five
Will you destroy it then?
I won't for the lack of five
But this place is full of sin

If there is but forty
Can the people live?
I will spare it for forty
For them I'm willing to give

Lord, be not angry
Please listen to me
Will you spare it for thirty?
Will you let them go free?

I will not destroy it for thirty
If that is what I see
Can you please spare this city
If you just find twenty?

I will not for twenty
May I speak once again?
Can you spare this place
If you only find ten?

I will spare it for ten
So the Lord went His way
Abraham was finished
With all he had to say

Both angels went to the city
To see what was going on
Lot was sitting at the gate
In a city where he didn't belong

He asked the two angels
To stay with him
They wanted to stay in the street
But he convinced them

Lot prepared a feast
He baked unleavened bread
The angels ate good
Before it was time to go to bed

The men of that city
Gathered around Lot's house
They wanted a relationship with the angels
That was reserved for a spouse

Lot tell us
Where are the men with thee?
Bring them out to us
They are men we want to see

Lot said to these men
Don't do so wickedly
I have two daughters
That I will let go free

They have not known man
They're virgins you see
But as for these men
They are staying here with me

They said to Lot, stand back
This fellow came in
And he is trying to judge us
On all of our sin

The men were so determined
They pressed Lot sore
The angels pulled him inside
And then they shut the door

The men were wicked
They were out of their mind
The angels smote them
So they wandered around blind

If you have family
Get them out of this place
The cry has waxen great
Before the Lord's face

Lot left the house
Speaking to who he saw
But he was as one that was mocked
By his sons-in-law

Early the next morning
The angels hastened Lot
Take your wife and two daughters
You need to leave this spot

Lot tried to linger
The angels took them by the hand
They put them out of the city
God was completing what he planned

Escape to the mountains
Do not look back
Don't stop and linger in the valley
You need to stay on track

Lot said to the angels
Oh no, not so
There is a city called Zoar
That's where I want to go

Since I have found favor
In the Lord's sight
I don't want to be overtaken by evil
I want to be treated right

I will accept this
Take your daughters and your wife
Do this right now
You're escaping for your life

After arriving in Zoar
Fire and brimstone hit the ground
Sodom and Gomorrah were destroyed
There was nothing to be found

I don't know what she was thinking
Must have been what she would lack
Lot's wife turned around
And start looking back

They had been warned
This was her own fault
While looking at the city
She turned to a pillar of salt

Early the next morning
Abraham went to the place
Where he discussed with the Lord
What Sodom and Gomorrah would face

Abraham looked at the city
Everything was destroyed on that plain
Because of their sinful nature
They had nothing to gain

God remembered Abraham
So He sent Lot out of the overthrow
It is not who you are
Sometimes it's who you know

Lot left Zoar
He and his daughter's went to a cave
This family didn't die
Look how God can save

The firstborn looked at the younger
Saying, Dad is very old
Then she made a suggestion
That I think was pretty bold

We can make Dad drink wine
He will give us what we need
Our family will not die
This will multiply our seed

The firstborn called her son Moab
Father of the Moabites to this day
The younger called her son Benammi
The Children of Ammon is what they say

The Widow's Oil - Read: II Kings 4:1-7

A woman cried to Elisha
My husband thy servant is dead
You know he was devoted
He made God his head

The creditors are coming
They are trying to take my boys
This would rob me
Of all of my joys

Elisha asked the widow
What can I do for thee?
What is in your house?
You can talk to me

The only thing I have
Is some oil in a pot
This family was very poor
They didn't have a lot

Gather some empty vessels
As many as you can
Borrow from your neighbors
They will understand

Once you get the vessels
Come home and shut your door
Fill them all the way
Until they take no more

Her sons brought the vessels
The widow got her pot
After she finished pouring
She still had a lot

She was told to sell the oil
To pay off her debt
The left over money is
What your family will get

This is what can happen
When you choose to obey
Don't become discouraged
God will make a way

NEW TESTAMENT

A Rich Man - Read: Luke 12:16-21

This story's about a rich man
Who thought he had it made
Look at what has happened
And the price that he has paid

His ground produced a large crop
This man was worried about space
I will pull down my barn
I will build a bigger place

This idea made him happy
His worries were over you see
He could build a barn so large
It would out shine you or me

Now I can kick back
I don't care what the future bring
I've provided for my life
I won't worry about a thing

This man was feeling good
He was acting calm and cool
God told this man
You are a fool

You have stored all of this stuff
Preparing for the future that you see
But did you know that on this night
Thy soul's required of thee?

Your thoughts are not on God
You think you did it all
When a man rises up so high
All he can do is fall

Now who is going to use
All of this stuff that you have stored?
This happens to the man
Who is not rich toward the Lord

The Alabaster Box - Read: Luke 7:37-50

There was a sinner woman
That knew Jesus sat at meat
She brought her alabaster box
And begin to anoint his feet

Jesus was invited to eat
With Simon the Pharisee
He invited him over
Without showing hospitality

The Pharisee was thinking
If Jesus is who He say
He would know about this woman
That touches him this way

Jesus knowing Simon's thoughts
Said, I want to speak to thee
Simon said to Jesus
You can speak freely

A creditor had two debtors
One owed five hundred pence
The other owed fifty
Both were on the fence

When they had nothing to give
He said, pay no more
This man had been a blessing
That was hard to ignore

The question I have for you
Should make no man boast
Which one of these men
Will love this man the most?

It's not the man
Who didn't owe much
The one that owed a lot
Is the one that he touched

Jesus told Simon
You selected the right one
Debt puts you in bondage
There's no place to run

Simon I came to your house
You provided no water for my feet
She used her tears and hair
Her task is complete

You gave me no kiss
She continues to kiss my feet
You didn't anoint my head
What she did was very sweet

This woman will be remembered
Her sins will be forgiven
Her faith has made her whole
She'll enjoy peaceful living

An Issue of Blood - Read: Luke 8:43-48

There was a woman
That had an issue of blood
She went to many physicians
Trying to end this flood

After suffering twelve years
She spent all of her living
The doctors couldn't cure her
But she kept on giving

She spotted Jesus
While in the multitude
Coming from behind
This woman pursued

She reached down
Touching the border of his clothes
Jesus asked: who touched me?
Nobody knows?

Peter said to Jesus
The multitude's pressing thee
Yet you are asking us
Who is touching me?

After she touched Jesus
The blood stopped flowing
She wanted to touch him
Without anyone knowing

When I was touched
Virtue left me
She came forth
So that everyone could see

The woman came out trembling
Sickness had taken it's toll
But after touching Jesus
She was made whole

She explained to everyone
What had occurred
About the money that was spent
And the cure that was preferred

Ananias and Sapphira - Read: Acts 5:1-10

Ananias and Sapphira
Came up with a plan
On a way to deceive God's church
On their parcel of land

During church giving
The couple kept back the full price
They could've given what they wanted
Were they making a sacrifice?

Peter asked Ananias
Why did you deceive the Holy Ghost?
What you gave was a blessing
No one's trying to boast

You were not lying to me
You were lying to the Holy Spirit
He knows your heart
When you lie He can hear it

Satan has filled thy heart
It is bad that you lied
After hearing this
Ananias gave up the ghost and died

About three hours later
Sapphira came strolling in
She had not heard about Ananias
Or the penalty for his sin

Peter asked Sapphira
What was the price?
She lied like her husband
This was not nice

Peter said to her
This is what the Lord will do
What has happened to Ananias
Will now happen to you

Sapphira fell dead at his feet
The men carried her out
Helping others when you're blessed
Is what giving should be about

We are all guilty of lying
This is what we do
Don't lie to the Holy Spirit
This could happen to you

Baby Jesus - Read: Luke 2:8-20

While shepherds kept watch
Over their flocks by night
God blessed them to witness
A wonderful sight

The Angel of the Lord came
The men were sore afraid
He told them where
The Christ Child would be laid

The Babes in swaddling clothes
Lying in a manger
There's nothing to fear
You are not in danger

Today, in the City of David
A Saviour's born unto you
The shepherds were probably wondering
What are we going to do?

Suddenly with the Angel
Came some Heavenly Host
Saying, Glory to the Highest
When worshipping God, It's ok to boast

They offered peace
And goodwill toward men
Christ has come
To save us from our sin

After the Angels left
The shepherds said to one another
Let's visit Bethlehem
Joseph, The Babe and his mother

Mary kept these things
Pondering them in her heart
The shepherd's returned praising God
They did their part

After seeing Jesus
They went to spread the Word
Praising the Living God
With all that had occurred

Dorcas - Read: Acts 9:36-42

Dorcas a loving disciple
As faithful as could be
Was full of good works
She gave all her gifts for free

She provided coats and garments
For the widows that she knew
Tabitha set a Christian example
The way we all should do

You can call her Tabitha or Dorcas
They are one in the same
It's just the interpretation
That changes her name

She became very sick
And died one day
Peter was asked to come quickly
Please do not delay

Peter went to the place
Where Tabitha was laid
He gathered all of the people
Then he kneeled down and prayed

Peter turned to her body
Telling her to rise
When he called her name
Tabitha opened up her eyes

Peter lifted her up
By giving her his hand
This miracle is known
Throughout the whole land

Feeding Five Thousand - Read: Luke 9:12-17

As the day was ending
While the sun was going down
The twelve disciples asked
Should the multitude stay around?

Shouldn't they go to the town and countries
That are very near
They can find food and lodging
There's nothing for them here

Jesus told the disciples
You can give them food to eat
But we only have five loaves and two fish
Shall we buy some meat?

Put them in groups of fifty
Have them sit on the grass
My God will make a way
To feed this hungry mass

There were lots of people
About five thousand men
The disciples were confused
So Jesus spoke to them again

Bring five loaves of bread
And the two fish
Jesus lifted His eyes to heaven
To multiply the dish

Everyone was full
Stomachs were very tight
When you trust Jesus
He will make everything right

Twelve baskets remained
After the meal was done
These people were blessed
They trusted God's Son

Good and Bad Seed - Read: Matthew 13:24-30

The kingdom of heaven is like a man
That sowed good seeds
While everyone slept, the enemy came
Planting a bunch of weeds

When the wheat start growing
The weeds start growing too
The servants asked their Master
What are we going to do?

Sir there were good seeds
Growing in your field
Why do you have weeds?
They worried about the crop being killed

While everyone was sleeping
The enemy had his way
Don't pull up those weeds
I'm going to let them stay

If you pull them now
The others may go to
I'm waiting for the harvest
That is what I'll do

Sometimes we are surrounded
By those ignoring God's will
Don't get upset or panic
Always remain still

Let them stay together
This will be just fine
When harvest time comes
I will claim what is mine

The weeds will be bound up
And thrown into a fire
They are getting burnt
Because Satan is a liar

The Good Samaritan - Read: Luke 10:29-37

A lawyer asked Jesus
Who is my neighbor?
Jesus told him a story
About a Samaritan that showed favor

A man left Jerusalem
On his way to Jericho
He was robbed by thieves
Always watch where you go

These men stripped off his garments
He was left half dead
The thieves tried to kill him
From what the bible said

A priest came along
That could provide
But when he saw the wounded man
He crossed to the other side

There was a Levite on the road
Walking the same way
He ignored the wounded man
He crossed the street that day

Then along came a Samaritan
Spotting the wounded man
He showed compassion
I will do what I can

He bandaged the man
Using oil and wine
With all that was done
The man would be fine

After putting him on his beast
Took him to an Inn
He continued nursing the stranger
That was beaten by these men

Before leaving the next day
He gave the Host two pence
To continue the man's treatment
Now that makes sense

If this is not enough
I will bring more when I come back
I want him taken care of
He should not lack

Jesus asked the lawyer
Of the three, who was his neighbor?
The lawyer replied, The Samaritan
He's the one that showed him favor

Jesus said to the lawyer
Go, and do the same
We are called Christians
When we act in Jesus name

Jesus Walks on Water - Read: Matthew 14:22-33

Jesus let his disciples
Get into a ship
I will take care of the multitude
It's time you take a trip

After taking care of the multitude
Jesus sent them away
He went to the mountains
And began to pray

When evening arrived
Jesus was all alone
The ship was being tossed by the sea
It was in a danger zone

Jesus went to the disciples
Walking on the sea
They thought they saw a spirit
Jesus said, No it's me

Do not be afraid
Peter said, Lord if it's you
I want to come to Thee
Is this something I can do?

Jesus told Peter
Yes, you can come
Peter got out of the ship
He was braver than some

Peter walked on water
Approaching the Lord
There was no mistaking
Who he was looking toward

Then he became distracted
The waves start pulling him down
You should never worry
Because Jesus is around

Peter start sinking and screaming
Master save me!
Jesus helped Peter and asked
Why do you doubt Thee?

Jesus and Peter got into the ship
The others begin giving praise
This trip was remembered
For the rest of their days

John Beheaded - Read: Matthew 14:1-14

Herod believed that Jesus was John
Risen from the dead
Great works have come forth
Since I've cut off his head

Herod had imprisoned John the Baptist
For Herodia's sake
John had warned Herod
About the wife he wanted to take

John told Herod
This is your brother Phillip's wife
You are disobeying God
By having her in your life

Herod wouldn't have John killed
He was very afraid
The people saw John as a prophet
A wise choice had been made

On Herod's birthday
Herodia's daughter danced for them
She was promised to the half of the kingdom
For pleasing him

Herod was probably shocked
By the request that she made
But, nevertheless
The price had to be paid

Herodia told her daughter
To ask for John's head on a platter
Herod didn't want to do it
But he attended to the matter

John's head was cut off
And delivered to her
This satisfied her mother
That wanted it to occur

John's disciples came
Taking his body away
After Jesus heard this
He departed, he didn't stay

Jesus got into a ship
After they decided to depart
He arrived at a desert place
Where the multitude touched his heart

John the Baptist - Read: Matthew 3

John was a preacher
That taught the Word of God
A bold soldier that went
Where others would not trod

John wore a leathern girdle
With raiment of camel's hair
His concern was for God's people
Not how much they stare

He ate a special diet
Of locust and wild honey
His heart was on serving God
Not on people's money

People came to John
To be baptized
He would lean them down
And then they would rise

The prophets had foretold
That John would come one day
Preparing God's people
With what he had to say

People came to see John
From all around
Looking for what was lost
Enjoying what had been found

The Pharisees and Sadducees
Heard what John said
These men didn't repent
They had a big head

John asked, Who warned you
Of the wrath to come?
When preaching to many
You can only reach some

You keep saying
Abraham is our father
He can't save you
Why do you bother?

The axe will be laid
Upon the root of the tree
If you produce bad fruit
You will not be free

I baptize with water
There's one mightier than me
He baptizes with the Holy Ghost
It's your sins that He can see

His fan is in His hand
He will purge His floor
He's gathering up His wheat
That will be with Him forever more

He will burn up the chaff
With unquenchable fire
Always follow Jesus
Because Satan is a liar

Jesus went to John
John wondered, how could this be?
I should be baptized by you
Yet you come to me

Suffer it to be so
Thus becometh us to fulfill
The purpose for all of this
Is to do our Master's will

John baptized Jesus
God's Spirit descended like a dove
This is my beloved Son in whom I'm well pleased
Was the message from above

Lazarus - Read: John 11:1-50

Lazarus was sick
Mary and Martha were upset
Let's contact Jesus
He's the one to get

They sent a message
He whom thou love is not well
The four were friends
Can't you all tell?

This is the same Martha
That kept her house so neat
And the same Mary
That anointed Jesus feet

Jesus said that Lazarus's death
Would glorify His Father
Do you think He rushed to him?
He didn't bother

He waited two more days
At the place where He was staying
Mary and Martha wondered
Why is Jesus delaying?

Jesus told his disciples
Let's go to Judea again
Master you were almost stoned
By those angry men

If a man walks by day
He will stumble not
But if he walks in darkness
He will stumble a lot

I'm going to wake Lazarus
Our friend is asleep
Jesus spoke about Lazarus's death
What He said was really deep

The disciple's didn't understand
They thought Lazarus was getting rest
This is good news
He will be at his best

Jesus told them plainly
Lazarus has died
I'm going to see him
I will be by his side

When Jesus was ready to leave
Thomas said, Let's go too
We can die with him
This is what we'll do

They told Jesus that Lazarus
Had been dead for four days
Learn to trust Jesus
Stop trying to understand His ways

The Jews comforted Mary and Martha
Because of their brother
This is a good example
Of people watching out for each other

After Martha heard that Jesus arrived
She went to Him and said
If you had been here
Lazarus wouldn't be dead

Jesus told Martha
Thy brother will live again
Martha knew about the resurrection
Happening in the end

Whatever you ask of The Father
I know He will surely give
Martha had great faith
That her brother was going to live

I am the resurrection and life
He that believes in me will live
He'll never die
Do you believe that life is what I give?

Yes, you are God's Son
You have come to save us
Martha went to see Mary
They had things to discuss

Mary didn't greet Jesus
She stayed home sitting still
Sometimes we do this
Not knowing how to feel

Martha told Mary
The Master has arrived
He's calling you
So she went to be by His side

When Mary left quickly
The Jews followed saying
She's going to Lazarus graveside
She'll weep where he is laying

When she saw Jesus
She fell at his feet and said
If you had been here
Lazarus wouldn't be dead

When He saw her weeping
And everyone that came with her
He groaned in His Spirit
Something was about to occur

Jesus told them all
Take away the stone
Martha said Lord he stinks
In a convincing tone

If thou would believe
You will see God's glory
What happened next
Will explain this awesome story

Jesus lifted his eyes
Saying, Father I thank thee
I know that You
Have heard me

There are people watching
I say this so they will see
That You are the one
That sent me

After He had spoken
He said in a loud voice
Lazarus come forth
Lazarus didn't have a choice

Lazarus came out
Bound by his grave clothes
He was alive
Now everybody knows

Jesus said, loose him
So that he can walk free
Some Jews start believing
The others ran to the Pharisees

The Pharisees and Chief Priest asked
What shall we do?
Jesus raises the dead
And does miracles too

Now if we do nothing
Many will believe
The Romans will take this place
We will have to leave

Caiaphas stepped forth saying
Ye know nothing at all
It's important that one man dies
So that our nation will not fall

Mary and Martha - Read: Luke 10:38-42

Mary and Martha are sisters
Lazarus is their brother
They are friends of Jesus
Watching out for each other

Jesus was going to teach
At Martha's house one day
He entered the village
Where He would stay

Jesus was teaching
God's Holy Word
I'm sure all the guest were excited
About everything they heard

Martha saw Mary
Listening to what Jesus said
Since she had been burdened with serving
A thought entered her head

Jesus, Mary is sitting
Shall I do this alone?
Bid her to help me
Martha replied with an angry tone

Jesus replied, Martha, Martha
Mary has chosen a needful part
She's not troubled
My Word will strengthen her heart

Never become so busy
Doing all that you do
You might miss a blessing
That's intended for you

The Prodigal Son - Read: Luke 15: 11-32

A Father had two sons
The youngest wanted his part
Of his Father's living
To make a new start

The Father divided the goods
Between the two boys
The youngest moved far away
To experience some joys

This boy took all of the money
That his Father gave
He spent it on riotous living
He did not save

There is no telling
Everything that he did
I know that harlots are involved
The details have been hid

After the money was gone
There was famine in the land
A citizen of that country
Tried to lend a hand

He let this poor boy
Feed his swine
This was a bad profession
It was out of line

The boy was so hungry
If he ate he would be fine
Maybe I should eat some of the husk
That I'm feeding to the swine

He start thinking about
How good the servants ate
I'm going home
Why should I hesitate?

I can talk to my Father
Tell him how I feel
If I become his servant
He will give me a meal

I will tell my Father
I've sinned before heaven and thee
I'm not worthy to be your son
Make a servant out of me

While at a distance
His Father saw him on his way
He ran and kissed his neck
They had plenty to say

I've sinned before heaven
I've sinned in thy sight
I shouldn't be your son
I didn't treat you right

The Father told his servants
Bring a robe, a ring
Some shoes for his feet
Kill the fatted calf so we all can eat

My son was lost
But has now been found
They had a great celebration
The eldest boy heard the sound

He asked a servant
What does this mean?
Your brother that was lost
Is now on the scene

The eldest got angry
He refused to go in
His dad came out
So they could talk like men

These many years
I've been faithful to thee
But you've never once
Killed a kid for me

But when your son arrives
You killed the fatted calf
He entertained harlots
He wasted his half

Son you are with me
What I have is thine
You've been faithful
You stayed in line

We must celebrate
Your brother was dead
But now he lives
Is what the Father said

The Rich Man and Lazarus - Read: Luke 16:19-31

There was a certain rich man
That wore purple and fine clothes
Lazarus is the beggar
That everybody knows

Lazarus laid full of sores
At the rich man's gate
If he could have a few small crumbs
It would be worth the wait

The rich man gave him nothing
But the dogs would lick his sores
If the rich man showed compassion
It would open many doors

After time passed
The beggar man died
God sent his angels
To be the man's guide

Lazarus was carried
To the bosom of Abraham
He received a promise
Made by the Great "I Am"

The rich man finally died
Lifting his eyes in hell
On earth he was exalted
But now he had fell

The rich man saw Lazarus
And Abraham from afar
He was tormented in a flame
While Lazarus was the star

The rich man cried, Father Abraham
Send Lazarus to help me
Some water would cool my tongue
I'm suffering, can't you see?

Remember your life
You received all that was grand
Now it's Lazarus turn
I'm sure you understand

Besides all of this
You're on a different side
Lazarus can't help you
This gulf is very wide

Well, since he can't come
Send him to my father's home
I have five brothers
That are starting to roam

If they won't listen to Moses or the Prophets
Or anything that's been said
Why would they take time
To listen to the dead?

Saul - Read: Acts: 9:1-18

This story's about a man
That consented when Stephen died
He didn't like the Christians
He wanted them killed or tried

There was persecution
Christians were scattered abroad
The Apostles stayed in Jerusalem
To worship The Living God

Stephen's body was buried
By very devout men
They mourned the loss of Stephen
And all that he had been

Saul tried to destroy the church
He entered every house
Anyone worshipping Jesus
Would be taken including your spouse

He dragged men and women
Putting them all in jail
Saul thought he was obeying God
He wasn't about to fail

Saul went to the High Priest
So he could get a letter
This would give him power
He could do his job much better

While on the road to Damascus
He saw a great light
Saul fell to the ground
Something wasn't right

Jesus asked Saul
Why do you persecute me?
Saul asked, who are you?
Jesus said, I Am Thee

It's hard kicking against the pricks
Saul asked, What shall I do?
Get up and go to the city
It will be explained to you

The men traveling with Saul
Couldn't say a thing
They heard a voice not knowing
The changes it would bring

When Saul got up
He was led by the hand
He had lost his sight
Things weren't going as planned

Saul lost sight for three days
He didn't eat or drink
We know that fasting
Makes it easier to think

The Lord spoke to Ananias in a vision
He said, I am here
Go restore Saul's sight
Do not fear

Ananias told the Lord
Saul is an evil man
He is trying to destroy Christians
Doing all that he can

Go, Saul's a chosen vessel
For the Gentiles and their Kings
Israel's going to benefit
From the knowledge that he brings

I will show him
The sacrifice that he will make
Saul is going to suffer
For my name sake

Ananias went to the house
Then he said Brother Saul
The Lord spoke to me
And I will explain it all

You met Jesus Christ
He appeared to thee
I'm laying hands on your eyes
So that you will be able to see

Saul was filled with God's Holy Spirit
It was like scales fell from his eyes
After he got up
Saul was baptized

This poem tells a story
Of how a man use to be
Saul was once blind
But now he could see

Sowing Seeds - Read: Matthew 13:3-23

Jesus teaches about a man
That went out to sow
Spread God's word
Where ever you go

While doing his work
He planted many seeds
If you want a good harvest
Beware of the weeds

Some fell by the wayside
The birds devoured them
Beware of Satan schemes
Jesus wants you to trust Him

The seeds that fell on stone
Sprang up very fast
Since they lack depth
These seeds will not last

When the sun comes up
They will get scorched
The crop will burn up
As if it were torched

Some seeds fell among thorns
These seeds got choked
While taking on the ways of the world
The gospel got soaked

The seeds on good ground
Yielded thirty, sixty, a hundred fold
These are faithful saints
Christians that are bold

Take God's word seriously
Don't ever fear
If you're a good listener
Be prepared to hear

Stephen - Read: Acts 6 & 7

The Grecians were complaining
Our widows are lacking food
The Hebrew's aren't treating them right
Should this be their attitude?

The twelve wanted to help
Without deserting the Word of God
We will appoint seven men
To go where we can't trod

The idea pleased the crowd
Stephen was chosen that day
The Apostles lay on hands
And they began to pray

God's Word increased
The Disciples multiplied
The Priest obeyed the faith
They were on the Lord's side

Stephen did wonders and miracles
But attracted a negative crowd
They rejected his spiritual wisdom
What he said was not allowed

He speaks against Moses and God
The false witnesses said
This Jesus is going to destroy the temple
And change the way Moses led

All that sat in council
Saw that Stephen had an angel's face
They looked at him intently
He was noticed in that place

The High Priest asked Stephen
Are these charges true?
Please listen to me
These men are deceiving you

The leaders are against me
Making an accusing sound
After Stephen's history lesson
No one wanted him around

After hearing what he said
They wanted to tear him apart
The truth is very painful
It cuts to the heart

Everyone cried out
Casting Stephen out of the city
They stoned him
The people showed no pity

The witnesses laid Stephen's clothes
At the feet of Saul
A man that hated Christians
With no compassion at all

Stephen looked into heaven
He was full of God's Spirit
He saw God's Glory with Jesus at his right
He didn't fear it

Stephen kneeled down saying
Lord receive my spirit
Stephen had a powerful message
But the people refused to hear it

Don't hold this sin against them
What he said was very deep
After he finished talking
Stephen fell asleep

The Ten Lepers - Read: Luke 17:12-19

On the road to Jerusalem
Passing through Samaria and Galilee
Jesus met people
That could represent you and me

While entering a village
He healed some leprous men
If I took count
I believe that there would be ten

The men lifted their voices
Calling Jesus by name
These men wanted to be healed
Why should they stay the same?

After Jesus saw them
He said, go see the Priest
All of them obeyed
From the greatest to the least

As they left Jesus
The leprosy went away
Jesus healed ten
But only one had something to say

The leper that returned
Was a Samaritan
He fell on his face praising God
He was a humble man

Jesus asked a question
Where are the nine?
I cleansed ten lepers
Standing in the line

The nine did not return
To give Glory to God
The only thing on their mind
Was the paths that they would trod

Jesus told the Samaritan
Your faith has made you whole
This stranger will enjoy peace
Not a troubled soul

Ten Virgins - Read: Matthew 25:1-13

The kingdom of heaven is like ten virgins
Five foolish and five smart
The foolish confessed with their mouth
But the wise believed in their heart

When you accept Jesus
You will receive His Holy Spirit
He is oil in your lamp
When darkness comes you will not fear it

The foolish virgins are people
That continue to play at church
The Holy Spirit is not within them
They don't know where to search

While traveling life's journey
Ten virgins slept and slumbered
When it was time to meet The Bridegroom
The foolish one's days were numbered

They wanted to share the oil
That the wise virgins had
A dry wick can only burn so long
Without oil it's pretty bad

People want what's yours
In the world this is what they do
When God gives the gift of His Spirit
It personally belongs to you

While the foolish went to find oil
The Bridegroom was the one the wise virgins met
Don't put off accepting Jesus
A closed door is what you'll get

After the foolish found oil
They start knocking at His door
Who is knocking, I don't know you
What are you knocking for?

Accept Jesus now
Don't continue to play like some
No one knows the day or hour
That Jesus is going to come

The Widow's Mite - Read: Mark 12:41-44

This story is about a widow
A poor widow with two mite
She pleased the Lord
By doing what was right

Jesus watched the people
By the treasury where he sat
Some were contributing this
Others contributed that

He noticed that the rich
Was casting in a lot
Then along came a widow
That gave all that she got

He called his disciples
He told what the widow had given
She gave more than anyone
Casting in all of her living

Wise Men - Read: Matthew 2

Jesus was born in Bethlehem
In the days of Herod the King
Wise men came to find Him
It's His praises they would sing

Where's the one that's born
King of the Jews?
After Herod heard this
He was troubled by the news

He asked the Priest and Scribes
Where will the birth be?
Bethlehem of Judaea
It's written in the prophecy

It's said that Bethlehem
Is considered the very least
The wise men said they saw His star
Shining in the East

Since Herod was troubled
He spoke to the wise men
When did you notice this star?
How long has it been?

Go find this child
This is something to pursue
Bring word to me
So I can worship Him too

After talking to the King
They followed the star leading the way
The wise men traveled
To where the child would stay

When they saw the star
They rejoiced with exceeding joy
They walked up to the house
Seeing Mary and her boy

They fell down and worshipped
Praising His name
The trip to see Jesus
Had nothing to do with their fame

The wise men gave Jesus presents
Of frankincense, myrrh and gold
They didn't go see King Herod
They didn't do as they were told

King Herod was very angry
They ignored what I said
They will pay the price
Kids two and under will be dead

An angel of the Lord
Appeared to Joseph in a dream
Telling him to flee Egypt
To avoid King Herod's scheme

Joseph woke up
Moving quickly that night
Herod had the children killed
It was a horrible sight

After the prophecy
Was completely fulfilled
There was weeping in Rama
Young children had been killed

An angel appeared to Joseph
After Herod was dead
You can return to Israel
Is what the Lord said

Joseph went to Israel
He was very afraid
Herod's son was no better
What kind of mess had he made

Being warned of God
He went to Galilee
He didn't want problems
He wanted to protect his family

This fulfills the prophecy
That remained to be seen
The Messiah that was coming
Would be called a Nazarene

Woman Caught In Adultery - Read: John 8:3-12

Early one morning
Jesus taught in the temple
People came to listen
Because He made the message simple

The Scribes and Pharisees
Came barging in
With a prostitute in hand
That had committed sin

This woman is a harlot
It's a well-known fact
Before we brought her to you
She was caught in the act

Now back in the day
Let me tell you what Moses said
A woman like this
Would be stoned dead

We brought her to you
To see what you thought
She is a harlot
That has been caught

Knowing they were tempting Him
Jesus stooped down
He took His finger
And start writing on the ground

They kept asking
He rose and said in a gentle tone
He who is without sin
Should cast the first stone

He stooped again
And continued writing on the ground
These men were convicted
They did not stay around

The men walked away
Leaving one by one
Convicted of their sins
And all that they had done

When Jesus stood up
The woman was there
She didn't know
That a man could care

Jesus asked the woman
Where are those that accuse thee?
Master, they're gone
They have abandoned me

Well neither do I
Go, sin no more
I'm the Light of the World
I'm here to restore

Zacharias and Elisabeth - Read: Luke 1:5-80

Zacharias and Elisabeth
Walked righteous in their days
They had no children
They were experiencing old age

During the time of Incense
People prayed on the outside
Priest could enter the temple
Anyone else would have died

Zacharias was in the temple
Burning incense was his lot
One day an angel appeared
In a special spot

Zacharias was very troubled
Standing at the altar in fear
An angel was on the right
Standing very near

Fear not Zacharias
Your prayers have been heard
Elisabeth will conceive
You can believe in God's Word

Zacharias asked the angel
How can this be?
We are very old
This is something I can't see

Since you don't believe
You won't speak until that day
You will walk around dumb
Without anything to say

All of the people marveled
Since he was in the temple so long
When he came out speechless
They didn't know what was wrong

Zacharias beckoned to them
He did this without speech
They didn't know what had happen
What conclusion could they reach?

After the Ministration
He went home and knew his wife
Elisabeth conceived
Bringing forth the promised life

Mary came to visit
Elisabeth was six months along
You can do anything
When God makes you strong

When Elisabeth heard Mary's greeting
The baby leaped for joy
This was Jesus's forerunner
Zacharias's boy

Mary went home
Before the baby came
Neighbors and cousins rejoiced
Giving Elisabeth fame

After eight days
His circumcision came
The people called him Zacharias
Elisabeth said, no John's his name

We have no kindred
By that name
Name him after his father
Their name should be the same

The people asked Zacharias
What will the baby's name be?
Zacharias started writing
A name for them to see

He used a writing table
To put the name on
My baby boy
Will be called John

Zacharia's mouth opened
Now his tongue was free
He start praising God
People asked, "What manner of child will this be?"

Zacharias was filled
With God's Holy Ghost
He explained God's prophecy
He didn't boast

John the Baptist grew
His spirit was very strong
He would preach in the desert
They wouldn't have to wait long

Acknowledgements

Giving honor to God who is the head of my life, I would like to thank Him for blessing me with this special gift. I thank my children Sarah, Elizabeth and Dillard IV along with my family and friends for their love and support.

CPSIA information can be obtained at www.ICGtesting.com
Printed in the USA
LVOW12s2146021214

416766LV00004B/10/P